CW01023179

Friend-SHIPS

The Incredible Things You Can Do To
Develop Amazing Friendships.

CHLOE WHITING

Disclaimer

This book is designed to provide information and motivation to our readers. It is sold with the understanding that the author and publisher are not engaged to render any type of psychological, legal, or any other kind of professional advice. The content is the sole expression and opinion of its author. Neither the publisher nor the individual author(s) shall be liable for any physical, psychological, emotional, financial, or commercial damages, including, but not limited to, special, incidental, consequential or other damages. Our views and rights are the same: You are responsible for your own choices, actions, and results.

The content of the book is solely written by the author.

DVG STAR Publishing are not liable for the content of the book.

Published by DVG STAR PUBLISHING

www.dvgstar.com

email us at info@dvgstar.com

NO PART OF THIS WORK MAY BE REPRODUCED OR STORED IN AN INFORMATIONAL RETRIEVAL SYSTEM, WITHOUT THE EXPRESS PERMISSION OF THE PUBLISHER IN WRITING.

Copyright © 2019 Chloe Whiting

All rights reserved.

ISBN: 1-912547-34-1
ISBN-13: 978-1-912547-34-0

DEDICATION

I want to dedicate my book to some special people in my life.

They are my Mum and Dad,
Gemma and Andrew Whiting ;
My siblings Leah, Moya and Jack Whiting;
Elise Trantum
My grandparents Debbie and Terry Smailes ;
Terry Whiting and Colin Whiting.

Also other family members:
Mark, Emma, Josh and Fynn Whiting ;
Paul and Catherine Whiting ;
Kristie and Ben Welch and Freya Whiting.

Finally my Grampy,
Philip Chan
aka The 10 Seconds Maths Expert,
who is An Award Winning Author
who helped and inspired me
with my learning and writing
this fabulous book.

Why did I write this book ?

Making friends is an important skill in life, whatever your age maybe and to know
HOW to make good friends can bring you fun
and happiness.

This is a lifelong skill which you will be learning all the time.

What you will learn from this book :

- How to understand Yourself First.
- How to make good lasting friends.
- Know why boys and girls think differently.
- How to deal with negative friends and people.
- How to communicate effectively with all your friends to bring out the best in them.

CONTENTS

FOREWORD i

ACKNOWLEDGMENTS iii

CHAPTER 1 1

THE FIVE LEVELS OF FRIENDS 1

CHAPTER 2 13

WHAT ALL PEOPLE WANT TO KNOW 13

CHAPTER 3 26

EIGHT TYPES OF PERSONALITY 26

CHAPTER 4 37

WHY DO GIRLS AND BOYS 37

BEHAVE DIFFERENTLY ? 37

CHAPTER 5 43

THE V.A.K OF COMMUNICATION 43

CHAPTER 6 60

THE TEN KEY STEPS IN MAKING AND KEEPING
GOOD FRIENDS 60

CHAPTER 7 70

THE IMPORTANCE OF SELF-IMAGE 70

CHAPTER 8 72

HOW CONFLICTS START AND RESOLVE IT. 72

CHAPTER 9 79

A CHECKLIST FOR MAKING FRIENDS 79

ABOUT THE AUTHOR..102

FOREWORD

"CHILDREN ARE OUR FUTURE"

Every child is UNIQUE and have been given talents.

We are born to succeed and with the right nurture and motivation, EVERY CHILD CAN DISCOVER THEIR UNIQUENESS.

I had the pleasure of working with a number of Children and Adult Authors and many initially did not believe they can ever write a book.

One of my youngest author, Amire Ben Salmi was age 4 when his book was published.

It was through the encouragement of his mother that he overcome his shyness and took action to become the youngest boy author in the world at the time of his publication.

I am so proud of Chloe wanting to write this book to be a better person and also along the way to share the knowledge to help and inspire other children to bring out the best of themselves.

There is a saying :

"PEOPLE DON'T CARE HOW MUCH YOU KNOW UNTIL THEY KNOW HOW NUCH YOU CARE!"

Well done Chloe making the effort to learn a lot of skills that will be useful to you and also to share this with you the Reader so you too can benefit from it.

Enjoy reading Chloe Whiting's book and please share.

Philip Chan
10 Seconds Maths Expert
Award Winning Author

ACKNOWLEDGMENTS

I am very grateful going to a number of events with my Grampy and meeting lots of wonderful positive and successful people and also I love making new friends.

I want to thank a number of people have been very encouraging and inspiring to me.

MAYOORAN SENTHILMANI
Co-owner of DVG STAR Publishing, Finance Director, Award Winning Author of 5 books, Inspirational & Empowerment Speaker. Thank you so much for helping me to publish my book.
www.dvgstar.com

LABOSSHY MAYOORAN
Co-owner of DVG STAR Publishing and wife of Mayooran Senthilmani's proud Wife, Mummy to 2 gorgeous boys
and Award-Winning Author of the book 'Mumpreneur '.
Thank you also for helping me to publish my book.
www.dvgstar.com

PRASANTHIKA MIHIRANI
Thank you so much for the wonderful design of my book cover.
She has helped so many Award Winning Authors with the design of their books. She lives in Sri Lanka.
You can contact her by email if you need her help
swissgraphics.mihiri@gmail.com

SABRINA BEN SALMI
Mother of the Fantastic Five.
She is Multi-Award Winning: MumPreneur, Author, Public Speaker & Business/Personal Development Consultant.

You can contact her by email : tmspp@yahoo.co.uk

THE FANTASTIC FIVE

LASHAI BEN SALMI

The oldest of the five. At only age 17, she is a Professional Speaker, Award Winning Author and her list of achievement take pages to list.

For example, Lashai's Youtube Channel (The K-WAY) to just under 20,000 subscribers and 3.1 million views.

TRAY-SEAN BEN SALMI

At age 13, he was in the top 20 finalist of Channel 4
Child Genius 2017. AS SEEN ON TV, RADIO & NEWSPAPERS Amazon No.1 Best Selling Co-author of : 10 Seconds To Child Genius.

He is known as ' I'm That Kid' and Tray-Sean is a Speaker, Mentor and Coach and already, like his sister, his list of achievements for such a young boy is so inspiring.

YASMINE BEN SALMI

At age 10, aka The LovePrenure and her amazing book, The Choice Is Yours. AS SEEN ON TV, RADIO & NEWSPAPERS, her list of achievement too is so amazing !

PAOLO BEN SALMI

At age 8, a published author, his book 'PINT Size Adventures'
He was one of the youngest person ever to interview
Dr John Demartini,a Human Behavioral Specialist and he is featured in the famous book, The Secret.
Paolo has been SEEN ON TV, RADIO & NEWSPAPERS

AMIRE BEN SALMI

At age 4, he was the youngest Boy Published author in the world.
AS SEEN ON TV & NEWSPAPERS, 5 years old, he is an

Award Winning Author and a Speaker.

DR DARI NANI
Owner/Director at MTN Media and thank you for all your help and inspiring me.

DR MARINA NANI
She is Woman of the Decade in Media.
Make the News on Radio TV Magazines Stage
Be seen Be Heard Be Present.
I want to thank her for giving me my very first Radio Interview on Radio Host of Radio WORKS World by KAT LORD.
Thank you to Marina MANI for inviting me to a number of her Red Carpet events and allowing me speaking at those events.
Thank you for your constant love and encouragements

KAT LORD, herself an Award winning Author of "There's More to Books than Reading", travel nanny and marathon runner!

.
PROFESSOR CHRIS O IMAFIDON
Professor Chris Imafidon, described by ABC News, and Fox News as world renowned consultant to Monarchs, Presidents, Governments and corporate leaders. Prof Chris Imafidon is a quoted authority by BBC, New York Times, Washington Post and CNN who has raised the highest number of Inner city child prodigies who became captains of Industries.
He is one of the most inspiring people I know and thank you for encouraging me.

There are so many wonderful people I have met at different events I have attended with my Grampy and many are very successful Business people, Authors, Professional Speaker, TV and Radio Presenters and other Top Professionals and friends like :

ANNETTE WHITE, LISA HAWKYARD, NICKY PETERS,
DR PAULINE LONG (SKY BEN238 TV).
FAYON DIXON (FORMER SKY TV).
JOHN AND BEVERLEY NEILSON,
RIMA ALEKSANDRAVICIUTE and so many others.
Thank you all!
PATRYCJA SURA, my good school friend.

Also to all my friends and Teachers at
Stopsley High School, Luton..

CHAPTER 1

THE FIVE LEVELS OF FRIENDS

Often people say: "This is my friend!"
In fact that's not really true because in real life today there are many people only have acquaintances.

Did you know that there are actually Five Levels of Friends ?

They are:-

LEVEL ONE
: Strangers
LEVEL TWO
: Acquaintances
LEVEL THREE
: Occasional friends
LEVEL FOUR
: Close friends
LEVEL FIVE
: Best friend(s)

Here is a brief explanation of each Level of Friends

LEVEL ONE - Strangers

Strangers are people that you don't speak to or know there name and they don't know anything about you.

Strangers are really friends you don't know yet.

For example

If you go to a friend's birthday party there may be people there you don't know yet.
However, when the party gets going you will start to play and talk to them and get to know them better.

Make a list of 5 Strangers you have met in the last 3 months
or
keep a note of Strangers you will meet in the next 3 months

1.

2.

3.

4.

5.

To turn Strangers into Acquaintances.

Here are some of the things you could to do as a starter (Examples):-

1. Find out their name

2. How old are they ?

3. About his/her family ? Any brothers and sisters

4. What do they like to do ?

5. Where do they live ?

6. Any interests or hobbies they have ?

   However, there is a much better way to remember how to start a conversation by using the **acronym**

   F . O. R. M. which stands for

   F : Family
   O : Occupation /Opportunity
   R : Recreation
   M : Money / Matter

You can use these in any order, or just one of them and see how your conversation carries on.

FOR EXAMPLE

FAMILY
You can asked them something related to their family or family members. In fact anything to do with the family.

OCCUPATION / OPPORTUNITY
You can ask them what their Mum and Dad do for a living, or if they have older brother(s) or sister(s) working.

Opportunity will depend on the situation, perhaps you both just miss the bus or train, or something that at that moment you have the same or similar experience.

Simple things like you both ordered the same ice cream flavour, or bought the same type of dress, shoes. It could be anything!

RECREATION
You can ask them about what hobbies they like the things they like to do like reading, dancing, listening to music or whatever.

MONEY

Everyone is talking something about money.
You can ask them : "Do you get any pocket money ?"
Do you like to go shopping with your parents ?
You can think of lots of other questions, anything to do with money.

YOUR GOAL is to get a conversation started and with practice and experience you will get better.
Be interested in the person you are talking to!

Once you have some rapport with the person, you can now move to Level Two.

LEVEL TWO – Acquaintances

What do we mean by Acquaintances?

Acquaintances are people you may see regularly and you may even know their name but you may not know very much about them yet.

For example
You see a lot of people at school and you might even know their name etc.
But you don't know what their likes and dislikes are.
They also might have different tastes say in : food , hobbies and music etc.

One of your goal could be either each day or each week, get to know one person you see often and start to talk to them for just 5 minutes.
And keep repeating this process.

Imagine what would happen over a year at school say for 40 weeks a year.
You could start to get to know so much more people!

Just to know my Acquaintances Better Plan

MONTH	Name of Acquaintance(s)	Where do I know then from
JANUARY	1. 2. 3. 4.	
FEBRUARY	1. 2. 3. 4.	
MARCH	1. 2. 3. 4.	
APRIL	1. 2. 3. 4.	
MAY	1. 2. 3. 4.	
JUNE	1. 2. 3. 4.	

JULY	1. 2. 3. 4.	
AUGUST	1. 2. 3. 4.	
SEPTEMBER	1. 2. 3. 4.	
OCTOBER	1. 2. 3. 4.	
NOVEMBER	1. 2. 3. 4.	
DECEMBER	1. 2. 3. 4.	

LEVEL THREE – Occasional Friends

These are the type of people you meet from time to time when
you go different clubs or activities in or out of school.

Examples like: A hockey or net ball club, a choir, a dance
or drama group etc.
These are the people you know a little bit more about them.

Just like you want to know your Acquaintances, you could do the same and get to know some of these people better by following the same or similar strategy.

LEVEL FOUR – Close Friends

Close friends are the people that you spend far more time with and do a lot more different activities together and you also learn a lot more about them and what they really like and dislike.

You talk to them a lot more than other people.

More importantly you have a lot more common interests.

There are many good books to read to help you, such as :

HOW TO WIN FRIENDS AND INFLUNCE PEOPLE
By Dale Carnegie

THE ART OF DEALING WITH PEOPLE
By Les Giblin

LEVEL FIVE – Best Friend(s)

It is very unlikely that most people would have more than a few best friends.

Some people in life don't even have a single one !

Best friends are the people that are always there for you and you can share secrets and thing you wouldn't tell anyone else. They are also there to help you get through hard times to cheer you up.

To have BEST FRIEND(S), it is NOT about having lots of them, it is not about the NUMBERS BUT THE QUALITY OF BEST FRIENDS.

If you have ONE BEST FRIEND that is better than having hundreds or thousands of Strangers or Acquaintances. Each one must decide for yourself what are the qualities you want in your Best Friend(s)

3 Keys Decision:

1. What do you Both Want ?
2. What will tolerate from your Best Friend ?
3. What will you not tolerate from your friends and will be both mutually agree ?

"IF YOU WANT TO FIND OUT
WHO ARE
YOUR TRUE FRIENDS.

WHEN YOU MESS UP
OR
WHEN YOU ARE GOING
THROUGH A DIFFICULT
TIME.

LOOK WHO WILL
STILL STICK
AROUND
FOR YOU!"

CHAPTER 2

WHAT ALL PEOPLE WANT TO KNOW

In this chapter you will learn about :-

- The PAIN-PLEASURE Syndrome

- The Six Human Needs

    (according to Anthony Robbins)

When you know why people do things, then you will know how to get along with them better.

The PAIN-PLEASURE Syndrome

There are important reasons why most people do things, it is mainly

BECAUSE :

**We either want to avoid PAIN or
Move towards doing things to give us
PLEASURE .**

For example :

Most kids don't like tidying up **(PAIN)**;
But we like to go and play with our toys **(PLEASURE)**.
Successful and smart people will be prepared to do the
important things even if it is not fun (Pain) and
that is the reason why they are successful.

On the other hand, unsuccessful people only want to do the
fun things in life, rather than the important things that may
not be fun.
So they often only achieve very little or end up poor.

Every person have a reason for what they do.
Even if they don't know why.
According to Tony Robbins,
He said basically there are 6 Human Needs.

These Six Human Needs are :-

1. **Certainty/Comfort Zone**
   The need for security, stability, and reliability.

2. **Variety/Uncertainty.**
   The need for change, stimulation, and challenge.

3. **Significance.**
   The need to feel acknowledged, recognized, valued and feel to be important.

4. **Love and Connection.**
   The need to love and to feel loved, and to feel connection with others.

5. **Growth.**
   The need to grow, improve and develop, both in character and in spirit.

6. **Contribution.**
   The need to give, to help others, and to make a difference.

When you understand what motivates people then you can adjust the way you deal with them to make them more comfortable with you, in the way you would interact with them.

This is a Lifetime skill that you will keep learning all your life whatever age you may be, if you want to get along with people and have good friends.

Certainty / Comfort Zone

One of the most important need for anyone is **Certainty**

Certainty is when you love to be right and never like being wrong.

Most people love to be right and not get things wrong but what a lot of people don't understand that making mistakes you're your learning and that you will actually learn more.

In fact, very smart people have made more mistakes then dumb people because they have gained far more experience by this.

If you look at some of the Greatest people in the world, they have made MORE MISTAKES than the people who have achieved very little in life.

My Grampy sometimes said:-

"There are 2 types of people who never make any mistakes.

One type are 'Dead' people and the other type are those people who do nothing with their life !"

For example, some of the Great achievers in History who have experienced great challenges and setbacks, like :

THOMAS EDISON
inventor of the Light Bulb

ALEXANDER GRAHAM BELL
the inventor of the telephone

ELI WHITNEY,
the inventor of the cotton gin

JAMES DYSON
the inventor of the vacuum and many more

MICHAEL HERSHEY
famous milk chocolate

THEODOR GIESSEL
 publisher and better known as Dr Seuss for Children's books

ALBERT EINSTEIN
mathematician and genius

OPRAH WINFREY
TV personality and TV Host

WALT DISNEY
famous Disney films and Theme Parks

Go and read about these people's story!

Variety /Uncertainy

Do you like surprises ?
If your answer is ' "YES"
You are really kidding yourself.

The reason is, you like the surprises of the things YOU
WANT
And the ones that you don't, people called them 'Problems !

Whilst it is good to have certainty life can be very boring.
So it is important to have some variety in life.
However some people who always wants to do a variety of
things in life but they never get a chance to finish of anything.
For this reason they never achieve anything of importance
even though they may be very skilled in life.

For example

A person may start to read a book and after a page or two
they check something or decide to call a friend and then
decide to watch TV and forget they were reading a book.

So if you have a friend that is like this they are consider as a
"jumping bean."
These friends can be very frustrating because if you were
starting to play a game and before you finish the game your
friend may say "I want to…!"

So you have to understand that this is what makes them
happy, so you have to make allowances for these people.

Significance

Significance means to feel important.
The question is HOW does a person do thing to make them feel important ?

On the negative side , people who are Bullies get their significance by hurting other people or making fun to upset other people. But really these are very insecure people and that is the reason why they do these horrible things !

On the positive side, Great people get their significance by doing thing to help other people and help others to be happier, or to inspire them to achieve more goal in life.

For example

I have a good friend, she is called Sabrina Ben Salmi and mum five kids and she gets her significance devoting all her time for her five children, to learn lots of positive and exiting thing in life.
They are called : The Fantastic Five.

In fact all her five kids are author and her youngest son Amires he is only four years old when his first book was published.
At that time, he was the youngest published author in the world.

So how do you get your significance?

Complete this for yourself :

I WANT TO GET MY SIGNIFICANCE BY

Love and Connection

According to Tony Robbins at one of his talks with several thousand people attending, he said :

"People will give up on their Goals and Dreams in order to meet their needs"

Love is like the oxygen of life and without it people dies mentally and spiritually.
It is what most people all want and need the most, whoever you are.

When we feel loved, we feel we can do anything.
But when you don't have love or lose love, we feel empty and dead inside.

For people who don't feel they get love from friends, family or anyone, some people will get a pet like a dog, cat, hamster etc
Because pet love unconditionally.

In the worst case they would hang around 'bad' people who gets into trouble because they feel 'belonging' to something.

The first four needs above :

Certainty. Variety. Significance, Love and Connections are often called

'The Needs of the Personality'

People will find their own ways to meet these need, whether it is good or bad.

For example

Some people will work very hard to avoid tackling the problems they have but will find excuses why they are doing it.

The last two Needs are often called :

'The Need of the Spirit'

Only a much smaller number of people in the world really do this.

These are two of the trait marks of very High Performer or Some of the people who have made the most contributions in the World, not only for themselves but for others like Mother Teresa.

Growth

It is very important for everyone in life to grow in different ways, otherwise they are dying mentally and physically.

For example

Lots of people when they get old they stop exercising their mind and body and that is why a lot of people's memories get worse. Also if they stop exercising then they would become weaker and may have problems walking and they may get fat by not exercising but it doesn't have to be anything hard.

Progress equals happiness.

The purpose of achieving is to help you get better and this is ongoing until the day you die.

Successful people will set goals every day in six key areas of their life: in Spiritual, Family, Work, Education, Money, Leisure and Health.

Contribution

For other people they get their significance by contributing in different ways, like helping to raise money for all kinds of charities like UNICEF, OXFAM, BRITISH RED CROSS etc.

For example

My grand Dad,I called him 'Grampy',
 Philip Chan is a supporter of UNICEF for over 50 years.
In fact he is an UNICEF Children's Champion and he is featured in UNICEF's official video.

For my contribution this is why I am writing this and every book sold I am going to give some money to UNICEF.
So that the money can be used by UNICEF to buy food and medicine for the poor people in the world.

What would YOU like to CONTRIBUTE to

....
....
....
....

Life is about creating MEANING that is important to YOU.

It is not only from what you are getting but also what you are giving to others.

**In the long term, it is not only what you get that will make you happy but rather
THE PERSON YOU BECOME AND WHAT YOU WILL CONTRIBUTE TO YOUR FAMILY, FRIENDS AND COMMUNITY.**

**When you know what is the <u>TOP TWO NEEDS</u> of a person's
6 Human Needs, you will understand a lot what will motivates them and why they behave in the way they do, whoever they are or whatever is their age.**

"BE A LAMPLIGHTER TO BRING LIGHT AND HAPPINESS TO PEOPLE WHO KNOWS ONLY DARKNESS AND UNHAPPINESS!"

CHAPTER 3
EIGHT TYPES OF PERSONALITY

We are all different but we are all creatures of **HABITS.**
These habits we have created and learned over a long period
of time.

We all have GOOD and BAD habits – some we know, some
we don't know and sometime we want to ignore our bad
habits even if it is not good for us !

Sometime we only know of our bad habits if it gets us into
trouble or someone tells us !

Here are some examples of Bad Habits, like :

Late for school;
Forgetting our books or homework;
Not bringing our PE kit to school;
Leaving our bedroom or family car in a mess;
Looking untidy etc.

I am sure you can make your own list of Bad Habits !

Different people have different personality.
We can broadly divide them into 8 types
(I want to give a big Thank You to my mentor Andy
Harrington,
 the World's Top Public Speaking Coach).

These are:-

Type One :
The Blamers
(or sometimes known as The Controller).

Type Two :
The Placater.

Type Three :
The Computer.

Type Four :
The Distractor.

Type Five :
The Warrior.

Type Six :
The Lover.

Type Seven :
The Saga.

Type Eight :
The Jester.

Let's try and understand the importance of knowing which type our friends belongs to and how we can use this information to make better friends.

TYPE 1: THE BLAMER
(Also known as the Controller)

Their main needs are :
SIGNIFICANCE then CERTAINTY.

A person with this type of personality are often scare to be wrong and always want to be seen to be right and when things don't go their way, in their thinking they always blame other person instead of looking at what they do.
They get their importance feeling to be right all the time and want to be in control.
In other word, they always want to be CERTAIN.

The reason they are like this is often because they have over bearing parents who failed to set boundaries and let them do what they want to do.
They are spoiled because as a child they don't really know what is right or wrong but their parent have not given them the guidance.

If you have friend with this type of personality, who is a BLAMER, then don't be surprised if they things goes wrong, they will blame others because they will not take responsibility for their actions.

TYPE 2: THE PLACATER
(Also known as the PLEASER)

Their main needs are :
CERTAINTY and CONNECTION.
People with this type of personality often take the 'Blame' for other people's mistakes, wrongly thinking they will be like more because of it.

They want to please people in the hope to accept them and sometimes people can take advantage of their good nature because they find it hard to say 'NO' !

They find it hard to make their own decision for themselves and put themselves under a lot of stress. This is why often these people get skin complaints and when they get older, if they can't break this habit have a greater chance of developing serious illnesses because of the stress they put on themselves.

Often it is because they have an over-bearing and controlling parent so they don't learn to make decisions for themselves.

They need to learn to be strong and learn how to say 'NO' !

TYPE 3: THE COMPUTER
(Also known as the Logical One)

Their main needs are :
CERTAINTY then SIGNIFICANCE.

This type of people like to be certain and hate to being wrong.
They think they are smart and logical in their thinking and perfect in their work.

They like to work by themselves and often get 'tunnel vision' and find it difficult to see the views and opinions of others.

They want to be 'Right' all the time !

Often this is the result of having parents who want to push them hard and being told what they are doing wrong and very critical without giving any praise first.

So they end up depending themselves with logic and reasons and start throwing facts and statistics at you !

TYPE 4: THE DISTRACTOR
(Also known as the Jumping Beans never stick to one thing)

Their main needs are :
VARIETY and SIGNIFICANCE.

These people are doing lots of things but never seems to finish anything.

For Example :

They may start making something but before they finished will do something else.
Or they star reading a book and after a few pages start reading another one.

They can seems to be very busy all the time but you can't trust them to finish off any tasks by themselves and this can be very frustrating for other people and themselves !

They hate to be wrong so when people challenges them they often will change the subject very quickly.

They are not very good listeners because they are busy talking to themselves.

TYPE 5: THE WARRIOR
(Also known as the Bold Action Taker)

This is the opposite of The Blamer.

They often point their finger when they are talking like a warrior holding a sword (their finger).

They are the leaders that calls people to take actions, participate and often will set new standards for others to follow.

These people just like to get on with the task rather just talking about it and are courageous, not worry to get things wrong.

They will fight for what is right and an inspirational Leader.

TYPE 6: THE LOVER
(Also known as the Giving from the Heart)

This is the opposite of The Controller.

This type of person makes their decisions from the heart.

They like working ,collaborating and connecting with people.

They sees the good in people and deeply caring in their nature.

In business, this type of person lobe to 'Network'

TYPE 7: THE SAGE
(Also known as the Wise One)

This is the lighter side of The Computer.

They like to know the truth and often very knowledgeable and wise.
They like to share their knowledge and often people ask then for their advice and speak very calmly and steadily.

They are hunger for the truth and want to share what is good with everyone.

TYPE 8: THE JESTER
(Also known as the Fun One)

This is the lighter side of The Distractor.

These people don't mind making fun of themselves and takes life very lightly.

There are the fun people and like to do things spontaneously.

They are full of energy and love to make people laugh and 'clowns' around.

Often the centre of attention at a party.

Thank you to ANDY HARRINGTON, Founder of the Professional Speakers Academy and Top UK Public Speaking Coach for teaching me these information.

"THE

BEST

MEDICINE

IS

LAUGHTERS!"

CHAPTER 4
WHY DO GIRLS AND BOYS BEHAVE DIFFERENTLY ?

Do you know why boys and girls behave differently?

Can you list ten things?

Just for fun, write it in the list below.

1.

2.

3.

4.

5.

6.

7.

8.

9.

10.

Scientists have found out that more boys have with behavioural problems then girls and this difference appears in early childhood.

This result comes from the latest data released from the study of Australian children.

The Australian's first nationally representative long-term study of child development involving almost 10,000 children from birth to nine years of age.

Of course you cannot say that for very every boy or girl, these are the general findings.

The average boy often with 'DO' first and then think about it , hopefully, second!

The average girl is more likely to think first and DO IT, hopefully, second.

Typically, boys has a much shorter concentration span that the typical girl. He gets easily bored and more likely to be disruptive when he is bored.

His verbal and literacy skills are weaker than girls. So too are boys' social skills and collaborative competencies. His listening skills are poor compared to girls.

Boys are less able to think reflectively, to plan and organise his work and follow step by step processes from start through to end with adequate attention to detail.

Girls, however, tends to be overly cautious and cares far too much details because they want to be perfect and get it right the very first time.

Interestingly, lots of experiments done by very smart people in Universities, that when a typical girl do something but determined to success, on their 5th attempt, over 80% of the time they will get it right!

I WILL SAY IT AGAIN! WHEN GIRLS KEEP GOING, ON THE 5TH TIME OF LEARNING SOMETHING NEW THEY ARE VERY LIKELY TO BE SUCCESSFUL!

How do we get our message or point of view across to people ?

Descriptive-Reflective-Speculative **(D – R – S) is how we communicate**.

It is also how we think and learn!

For example :-

Let's look at why some people gets Bullied !

DESCRIPTIVE
"Over 90% girls in Year 7 get bullied by older pupils! Why?"

REFLECTIVE
"Perhaps when they are new or lacking in confidence they are easy target or older pupils with poor self-image of themselves want to feel powerful by bullying younger pupils? "

SPECULATIVE
"What happen if each Year 7 pupil particular girls have a Buddy Partner with pupils in Year 11.
Maybe this could help to prevent the problem because by then the Year 11 should be more responsible!"

Research shows that Boys and Girls learn at different rate, especially between the age of 11 -16 but then by the time about 18 their learning rate are similar and boys start to catch up to girls.

At school, particularly from Year 7 to 9,the subjects that are Boy Friendly is often different from Girl Friendly subjects.
This is for the majority but may not be true for every single boy or girl.

BOY-FRIENDLY SUBJECTS
Maths
Physics
Physical Education

GIRL-FRIENDLY SUBJECTS
English
Modern Languages
Religious Education
Music
Art
Drama
Biology
Chemistry
Integrated Humanities (Religious Education, Geography and History)

SUBJECTS FRIENDLY BOTH GIRLS AND BOYS
History
Geography
Technology

Thank you to Professor Geoff Hannah for this work.

"IT IS OKAY
TO HAVE
DIFFERENCE
OF OPINIONS.

RESPECT
OTHER'S POINTS
OF VIEW

YOU DON'T HAVE TO
AGREE WITH PEOPLE ALL
THE TIME!"

CHAPTER 5
THE V.A.K OF COMMUNICATION

How to develop Rapport with Anyone

Rapport means how to get on with people.

How do we Learn ?

A very clever man by the name of Howard Gardner did a lot of study watching people and he found out some very interest things.

He said, there are seven different learning styles:

Auditory

Visual,

Kinesthetic

Interpersonal,

Intrapersonal

Linguistic

Logical-mathematical.

My Grampy is a Professional NLP Coach and he is teaching me these skills.

He said to learn it properly will take a life time, so start simple from the first three :

Visual

Auditory

Kinesthetic.

What is NLP ?

NLP stands for Neuro-Linguistic Programming.

It is the way how we use our spoken language and our Body Language to communicate with other people that helps us to make good connections.

The VAK learning style uses the three main sensory receivers:

Visual, Auditory, and Kinesthetic (movement) to determine the main way we learn best.

It is also sometimes known as

VAKT

(Visual, Auditory, Kinesthetic, & Tactile)

Hints for Recognizing and Implementing the Three VAK Styles

Visual learners

People who are visual learners they think in pictures so they love seeing diagrams.

They remember colours, shapes, and forms.

"A picture paints a thousand words"

The other way you can tell someone who is a visual tend to talk very quickly.

Auditory learners

often talk to themselves. They also may move their lips and read out loud. They may have difficulty with reading and writing tasks. They often do better talking to a colleague or a tape recorder and hearing what was said.

Visual learners have two other ways known as *linguistic* and *spatial*.

Learners who are *visual-linguistic* like to learn through written language, such as reading and writing tasks.

They remember what has been written down, even if they do not read it more than once.

They like to write down, say the directions and pay better attention to the task if they watch them.

Learners who are *visual-spatial* usually have difficulty with the written language and do better with charts, demonstrations, videos, and other visual materials.

They easily visualize faces and places by using their imagination and seldom get lost in new surroundings. To integrate this style into the learning environment:

- o Use graphs, charts, illustrations, or other visual aids.
- o Include outlines, concept maps, agendas, handouts, etc. for reading and taking notes.
- o Include plenty of content in handouts to reread after the learning session.
- o Leave white space in handouts for note-taking.
- o Invite questions to help them stay alert in auditory environments.
- o Post flip charts to show what will come and what has been presented.
- o Emphasize key points to cue when to takes notes.
- o Eliminate potential distractions.
- o Supplement textual information with illustrations whenever possible.
- o Have them draw pictures in the margins.
- o Have the learners envision the topic or have them act out the subject matter.

Kinaesthetic learners

Kinaesthetic learners have trouble listening or reading instructions.

They just to get on and to the task and as a result they often get things wrong.

The way you can tell a kinaesthetic person is that they tend to talk very very slowly and this can be very annoying to other people.

When you talk to these type of people then talk very slowly and that would make a good impression on them.

The way to get on with visual people they like you to talk quickly and also in your convocation with them use lots of visual words.

They do best while touching and moving.

It also has two other ways: kinesthetic (movement) and tactile (touch).

They tend to lose concentration if there is little or no external stimulation or movement.

When listening to lessons they may want to take notes for the sake of moving their hands.

When reading, they like to scan the material first, and then focus in on the details (get the big picture first).

They typically use colour high lighters and take notes by drawing pictures, diagrams, or doodling.

To make the most of this style into their learning :

- o Use activities that get these people to move.
- o Play music, when appropriate, during activities.
- o Use colour markers to emphasize key points on flip charts or white boards.
- o Give frequent stretch breaks (brain breaks).
- o Provide toys such as Koosh balls and Play-Dough to give them something to do with their hands.
- o To highlight a point, provide gum, candy, scents, etc. which provides a cross link of scent (aroma) to the topic at hand (scent can be a powerful tool).

VAK Survey

Read each statement carefully. To the left of each statement, write the number that best describes how each statement applies to you by using the following guide:

1	2	3	4	5
Almost Never	Once in a While	Sometimes	Often	Almost Always

Answer honestly as there are no correct or incorrect answers. It is best if you do not think about each question too long, as this could lead you to the wrong conclusion.

Once you have completed all 36 statements (12 statements in three sections), just add up your score in the spaces provided.

Section One - Visual

_____ 1. I take notes and/or draw mind maps.

_____ 2. When talking to someone else I have a difficult time understanding those who do not maintain good eye contact with me.

_____ 3. I make lists and notes because I remember things better if I write them down.

_____ 4. When reading a book, I pay a lot of attention to passages that help me to picture the clothing, description, scenery, setting, etc.

_____ 5. I need to write down directions so that I can remember them.

_____ 6. I need to see the person I am taking to in order in order to keep my attention focused on the subject.

_____ 7. When meeting a person for the first time, I notice the style of dress/clothes they are wearing first.

_____ 8. When I am at a party, one of the things I love to do is stand back and see what is going on.

_____ 9. When remembering information or places, I can see it in my mind.

_____ 10. If I had to explain something new to someone, I would prefer to write it out.

_____ 11. In my free time I am most likely to watch television or read.

_____ 12. If someone has a message for me, I am most comfortable when they sends me a text.

Total For Visual _____ (note: the minimum is 12 and maximum is 60)

Section Two - Auditory

_____ 1. I read out loud or move my lips to hear the words in my head.

_____ 2. When talking to someone, I have a difficult time understanding those who do not talk or listen to me.

_____ 3. I do not take a lot of notes, but I still remember what was said. Taking notes often puts me off from listen to other people.

_____ 4. When reading a book, I take a lot of attention to the passages involving conversations, talking, speaking, dialogues, etc.

_____ 5. I like to talk to myself when solving a problem or writing or working things out.

_____ 6. I can understand what someone says, even if I am not focused on the person themselves.

_____ 7. I remember things easier by repeating them over and over.

_____ 8. When I am at a party, one of the things I love to do is talk a lot about things that is important to me with a good conversationalist.

_____ 9. I would rather receive information from listening from someone explaining, rather than read a text or book.

_____ 10. If I had to explain how something new works, I would prefer talking about it.

_____ 11. With my free time I am most likely to listen to music.

_____ 12. If my teacher/friends/adults has a message for me, I would prefer they talk to me or call me on the phone.

Total For Auditory _____ (note: the minimum is 12 and maximum is 60)

Section Three - Kinesthetic

_____ 1. I am not good at reading or listening to directions. I would rather just start working on the task or project given to me.

_____ 2. When talking to someone, I have a difficult time understanding those who do not show any kind of emotional or physical support.

_____ 3. I take notes, doodle, and/or make mind-maps, but I rarely go back and look at them.

_____ 4. When reading a book, I pay a lot of attention to passages revealing feelings, moods, action, drama, etc.

_____ 5. When I am reading, I move my lips.

_____ 6. I often exchange words, such as places or things, and use my hands a lot when I can't remember the right thing to say.

_____ 7. I normally appears disorganized.

_____ 8. When I am at a party, one of the things I love to do is enjoy joining in the activities such as dancing, games, and totally losing myself in doing the activity.

_____ 9. I like to move around. I feel trapped when seated for a long time or at the same spot.

_____ 10. If I had to explain a new ways to do things, I would prefer actually demonstrating it and showing it to people.

_____ 11. With my free time I am most likely to exercise.

_____ 12. If people has a message for me, I am most comfortable when they talks to me in person.

Total For Kinesthetic _____ (note: the minimum is 12 and maximum is 60)

Total each section and place the sum in the blocks below:

VISUAL	AUDITORY	KINESTHETIC
number of points: _____	number of points: _____	number of points: _____

While you may prefer to learn by using the method with the highest score, you will find that normally learn best by using **all** three to help you learn better.

"IN LIFE
WE CAN LOOK
AT THE
SAME THING
BUT
DON'T ALWAYS
SEE
THE SAME THING !

SAME
LOAF
DIFFERENT
SLICES!"

CHAPTER 6

THE TEN KEY STEPS IN MAKING AND KEEPING GOOD FRIENDS

1. KEEPING YOUR PROMISES

2. BE DEPENDABLE

3. APOLOGIZE WHEN YOU'VE MADE A MISTAKE

4. ALLOW YOURSELF TO BE HONEST AND VULNERABLE

5. DISAGREE WITH YOUR FRIEND IN A RESPECTFUL WAY

6. DON'T USE PEOPLE

7. BE LOYAL

8. BE RESPENTFUL

9. DO NOT LET YOUR FRIENDS FEEL LEFT OUT, EVER

10. BE SELFLESS

Notes

1.   Keeping your promises

You want to be known as a trust worthy person so only make a promise that you can keep.
However there will be time because of circumstance that you may not be able to keep that promise.
For example.
Let's say you promise to visit a friend far away and you can only get there by train and there was a Train Strike, or say we had very heavy snow and there was no way you could get to your friend.

2.   Be dependable

This is one of the most important quality of a person, especially as a good friend.
People hate having fake friends if you are not a dependable person and keep letting people down,
very soon people will start to avoid you.

3.   Apologize when you've made a mistake

Everyone in life will make a mistake some times.
Great and mature people are not afraid to admit when they are wrong and will apologize when they have made a mistake.
Big people do not hesitate to apologize when they are wrong and not blame other person.

4.   Allow Yourself To Be Honest and Vulnerable

No one is perfect and some times and we can unintentionally hurt other people's feelings.

Or, other people can hurt our feelings too.

No one can be good at everything and that is fine.

So when you're not good at something don't try to hide it and be honest. People will appreciate your honestly.

Because you are being real.

Don't be a 'KNOW IT ALL' type of person because they will think you are a Big Head !

People like REAL people not fakes !

5.   Disagree with your friend in a respectful way

Everyone have opinions and also people can see different things and sometimes people miss things.

For example

If you see a glass which is filled half way.

Some people may say it is half full, whilst other people will say it is half empty.

Now some people say if you see it as half full then you have a positive attitude.

Whilst other people will see it as half empty, are said to have a negative attitude.

The truth is ,neither of them are right or wrong.

That is just the way they see it and that's it !

Unfortunately people decide to attach an emotional judgement to it when it is totally not necessary !

It is okay to have different points of view and not to judge for their opinion.

6.   Don't use people

People are valuable. Appreciate people and their acts of kindness.

There is a saying :

"Use things and appreciate people NOT use people and appreciate things"

People who uses people are not honest people and are very selfish and manipulating.

They don't really care about anyone other than themselves.

Stay away from these people who called "Friends!"

7.   Be Loyal

Being loyal is an important skill in life because people can trust you with their secrets and thoughts.

Also, they know they can depend on you.

Sticking by your friends is important.

For example

Let's say you promised to go to your friend's birthday party but someone often you to go on an expensive trip.

What do you think a 'loyal' friend would say?

8.   Be respectful

There are many different ways to be respectful, such as :

Removing your shoes when entering someone else house;

Or wait until everyone is seated at the table before you start to eat;

If you friend can't eat certain type of food, or don't like listening to certain types of music. When they are with you, then don't do things that they don't like even deep down you want to !

Boys can show good manners by opening a door for girls or people older to get first;

Helping old people across the road;

Or keep quiet when you are in the library etc.

JUST BE THOUGHTFUL !

CAN YOU THINK OF MORE EXAMPLES FOR YOURSELF ?

Things to do to be respectful (Make up your own list) :

#1.

#2.

#3.

#4.

#5.

#6.

#7.

9.   Do not let your friends feel left out, ever!

WE ALL WANT TO BELONG TO SOMETHING!

To be in a Group of Friends therefore is very important but only if they are good and respectful and not in Gangs that do bad things.

Never leave your friends out because it is unkind and it would make them feel unwanted and that is not a very nice thing to do.

Try and get all your friends to participate and if they are not good at something, encourage them to have a go at it!

For example

If you were at school and you was playing a game and a person came up to you and asked if she could play with you to and you said "this game has a limited amount of players" and lied.

That is not an action of a true friend.

Please never do this! This is a form of Bullying!

Big and caring people never do this!

10.   BE Selfless

Being SELFLESS is when you think of others before you think about yourself and you have got their interest at heart because you really care.

There is a very famous saying

"PEOPLE DON'T CARE HOW MUCH YOU KNOW UNTIL THEY KNOW HOW MUCH YOU CARE!"

People like people who really care about people!

"THE "MIRACLE IS THIS – THE MORE WE SHARE, THE MORE WE HAVE!"

Leonard Nimov
(Actor of Star Trek series)

CHAPTER 7
THE IMPORTANCE OF SELF-IMAGE

What is Self-Image?

It is simply the way we see and think about ourselves.

Which means that if you think you are not very good at doing something, for example, doing mathematics then you always condition yourself not to be good at doing maths so you don't try as hard.

Many people don't even get started.
The truth is if they just get on with the task they actually find most of the time it is much easier than they think.

This is a very important statement that all of us need to understand and remember :

"ALL OF YOUR THINKING AND ACTIONS ARE ALWAYS CONSISTENT WITH THE SELF-IMAGE YOU HAVE OF YOURSELF"

We often find that people with poor self-image often achieve very little. Even though often they have great natural talents and abilities because of their poor self-image they tend to waste their talents.

On the other hand, people with a good self-image will achieve far more because they are not afraid of making mistakes.

So they will do and try lots of things and in the long run they will achieve more.

Five steps to change your self- image

1.You need to know the image you have of yourself was made in error ! It's the feeling that form the image – not the real facts .
2.Since it is a mistake it can be changed.
3.Decide who it is that you want to be .
4.Write them down on a piece of paper .
5.Spend time with that person you want to be every day.

In the last chapter of this book we will look at some affirmations.

Learn to accept and forgive yourself.
Don't be so hard on yourself!
Always speak kindly to yourself about you.

CHAPTER 8
HOW CONFLICTS START AND RESOLVE IT.

UNDERSTANDING THE CONFLICT CYCLE.
(CREATED BY DR ANGELO NARDONE)

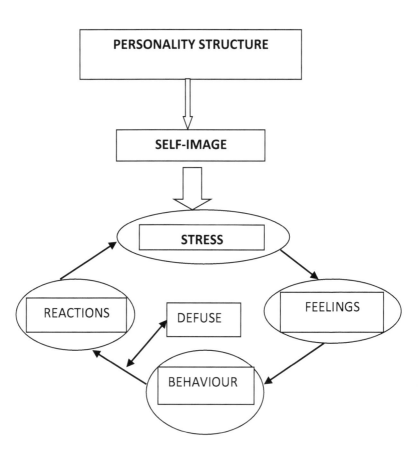

Here is how the Conflict Cycle Model works.

Feelings
is what stress does for you.

Behaviour
is the way we react to our feelings.

Reaction
is the way a person reacts to your bizarre **behaviour**.

WHAT IS STRESS ?

Pressure is external outside of you !

When you internalize it, meaning you start talking to yourself, you put yourself under pressure then it becomes Stress
.
Stress can be positive or negative.
It is all depending on your attitude and Self-image.

For example,
Ice-skating, Rock climbing, sky diving , performing on front of an audience etc

Can you think of five different thing that would be quiet challenging ?

1.

2.

3.

4.

5.

There are four types of stress :-

1. PHYSICAL

2. PSYCHOLOGICAL

3. REALITY

4. DEVELOPMENTAL

Types of stress	Examples
Physical	Sleepy, hungry etc
Psychological	Personal threats, rejections, unrealistic goals etc
Reality	Late for appointments, missing a bus or trains, late for lessons or appointments etc
Developmental	Starting a new task, meeting new people, having to make a speech. Or simply learning something new for the first time.

When you are learning anything new, it doesn't matter who you are or whatever age you are, you have to go through four stages.

Here are the Four Stages of Learning

Stage one:
Unconscious Incompetence

Stage two:
Conscious Incompetence

Stage three:
Conscious Competence

Stage four:
Unconscious Competence

How the Four Stages of Learning works

Unconscious Incompetence

This is the stage WHEN YOU DON'T KNOW WHAT YOU DON'T KNOW.

For lots of people without the help of a mentor or coach they will give up because they will make so many mistakes without any success. Also that can waste a lot of time and money.

Conscious Incompetence

This is the 'MAKE OR BREAK' Stage.

When they have a little bit of knowledge, for example when someone learns how to drive and they have had a few lessons. They can do it but not very well and have to think about every stage they are doing.

Conscious Competence

This is the ' I CAN DO THIS' Stage.

Because you have done a lot of practice of whatever you have been learning. You are now getting very good at it but you still have to think about what you are doing.

Unconscious Competence

This is the 'I AM GREAT AND I CAN DO THIS EASILY' Stage.

Because you have done so much practicing of the skill, for example when people who have been driving for a long time or doing the same job for many years. They almost do it automatically.

So it is important to go through these four stages.

"THE BEST TREASURES ARE FINDING TRUE FRIENDS"

CHAPTER 9
A CHECKLIST FOR MAKING FRIENDS

Personal Quality List

KNOW YOURSELF FIRST!

Here is a list may to help you to GET TO KNOW YOURSELF !

Tick off which ones that describes YOU !

Please take your time if you really want to know yourself better.

"Successful people will do the things Common people won't do!"

Another really famous saying :

"Successful people will do the COMMON THINGS UNCOMMONLY WELL!"

THINGS THAT WORTHWHILE ACHIEVING TAKES TIME!

When you become the Better version of YOU, then it is so much easier to make Good Friends and be attractive to other people.

There are some very BIG WORDS you may want to find out what they mean. Ask your parents to help you, use a dictionary, or Google it !

To help you, Pick the top 10 qualities do you want to work on to improve yourself !

1. Accepting
2. Accommodating
3. Affectionate
4. Affirming
5. Agreeable
6. Alluring
7. Altruistic
8. Ambitious
9. Amiable
10. Analytical
11. Appreciative
12. Articulate
13. Assertive
14. Attentive
15. Authentic
16. Balanced
17. Candid
18. Careful

19. Caring

20. Cheerful

21. Comforting

22. Communicative

23. Compassionate

24. Competent

25. Congenial

26. Conscientious

27. Cooperative

28. Courageous

29. Creative

30. Decisive

31. Diplomatic

32. Discreet

33. Easy going

34. Educated

35. Effective

36. Efficient

37. Encouraging

38. Enthusiastic

39. Extroverted

40. Flexible

41. Forgiving

42. Forthright

43. Friendly

44. Frugal

45. Genuine

46. Godly

47. Graceful

48. Growing
49. Hard working
50. Helpful
51. Honest
52. Humble
53. Humorous
54. Imaginative
55. Industrious
56. Insightful
57. Intelligent
58. Intuitive

My Best 10 Qualities to work on myself

1.

2.

3.

4.

5.

6.

7.

8.

9.

10.

"TRUE FRIENDS ARE NEVER APART. MAYBE IN DISTANCES BUT NOT IN THEIR HEART."

CHAPTER 10
THE IMPORTANCE OF AFFIRMATIONS

SOME WILL – SOME WON'T – SO WHAT !

What is Affirmations?

According to the Concise Oxford Dictionary.

'Affirming', especially in law is a solemn declaration by a person to be true, which mean you are saying thing you believe to be TRUE !

So affirmations are things you will say to yourself and you want to do it every day !

Affirmations are dynamic and practical—not wishful thinking.

IDEALLY, AFFIRMATIONS SHOULD BE REPEATED IN A QUIET PLACE WITH NO ONE AROUND..
THIS REPETITION WILL HELP TO CHANGE YOUR HABITS AND ATTITUDES OVER WHICH ONE NORMALLY HAS LITTLE CONTROL.

DO NOT UNDERESTIMATE THIS SIMPLE ACTIONS THAT CAN CHANGE YOUR LIFE !

TRIED these POSITIVE AFFIRMATIONS TO help you to MAKE FRIENDS

1. I have a positive vibe that attracts a positive friends

2. Every day is a new opportunity to make new good friends

3. Making new friends comes easily to me everywhere.

4. Having close friends is a very important to me

5. Every day my circle of good friends grows

6. All of my friendships are real and we have a great time

7. Every day I welcome more friends into my life

8. I am the Best Friend anyone can have

9. My friendship circle brings happiness to me and others

10. I am grateful each day for all of my wonderful friends

Affirmations need to be personal to you and relevant to what you are trying to achieve.

Once you have made your positive affirmations, keep it where you can easily find to it whenever you want to use it.

Many successful people use Affirmations in their life every day to keep themselves positive and to achieve the things they want to achieve, even when other people are telling them they can't do it !

Make sure to start each day with your positive affirmations and look at them when you need them. They will really keep you positive and attractive.

Life is a Choice – Some Will, Some Won't, so what!

Take charge and make 10 Affirmations for yourself so it is personal to you ? Do it and have fun!

1.

2.

3.

4.

5.

6.

7.

8.

9.

10.

Life is a CHOICE.

If you want to be successful then follow what successful people do !

SOME WILL......SOME WON'T........

SO WHAT !

ONLY YOU CAN MAKE THE DECISION FOR YOURSELF.

"THERE IS NO SUCH THING AS PROBLEMS, ONLY CHALLENGES AND OUTCOMES"

FACTS YOU MAY NOT KNOW!

Facts lots of people don't know that many of the Famous Celebrities today was once badly bullied when they were at school !

Here is just a small list of famous people who were bullied very badly but managed to be successfully despite lots of pain and griefs and overcome their bullies and now they have amazing careers and lifestyle today.

Remember your school days is one part of your life NOT the whole of your life !

These people have turned their PAINS into SUCCESS, SO CAN YOU !

Beautiful actresses like Megan Fox, Mila Kunis,

Sandra Bullock and Emma Watson.

Even USA Presidents like Bill Clinton and Barack Obama had their share of their 'friends' being nasty to them as children.

Famous film maker like Steven Spielberg managed to use these horrible experience to his advantage by creating creative stories to help people today.

Many Rich and Famous people were badly bullied at one time early in their life.

Here are some examples

Megan Fox

Megan Fox said that she felt that high school would never be over as she faced constant bullying at school.

She is age 30.
Profession: Model, Actor
Some of her works : Transformers, Transformers: Revenge of the Fallen, Teenage Mutant Ninja Turtles, Jennifer's Body

Christian Bale

He started acting at 13. Because he was young, his classmates used this as a reason to bully and beat him. But he stayed strong and he went on to play Batman.

He is age 43
Profession: Actor, Voice acting
Some of his works: The Dark Knight, The Prestige, American Psycho, The Dark Knight Rises

Mila Kunis

Mila Kunis was bullied in school because of her "funny face." The *Black Swan* star says that kids would make fun of her big eyes and lips.

She is age: 33
Profession: Model, Actor, Voice acting
Some of her works: Black Swan, That '70s Show, Ted, Friends with Benefits

Rihanna

She says that she was teased in school for the colour of her skin being a Black person and her breasts.

Rihanna says she is grateful for these struggles because they made her stronger and better person.

She is age: 29
Profession: Fashion designer, Songwriter, Actor, Music artist, Singer
Some of her works: The Hangover, Wreck-It Ralph, 21, I Love You, Man

Chris Rock

He is the 'funny' man and he says developed his humour and wit as a tool to response to bullies.

He is age: 52
Profession: Comedian, Television producer, Film Producer, Screenwriter, Actor, + more
Some of his works: Chris Rock: Bigger & Blacker, Madagascar, Head of State, The Oscars

Jessica Alba

Even though Jessica Alba is very successful and a beautiful actress, but the *Sin City* star was bullied in high school. Jessica said she got picked on because she was an awkward child with buck teeth and a Texas accent.

She is age: 35
Profession: Model, Actor
Some of her works : Sin City, Fantastic Four, Fantastic Four: Rise of the Silver Surfer, Valentine's Day

Jennifer Lawrence

Jennifer said that she was so badly bullied that she switched schools to get away from them.

She is age: 26
Profession: Film Producer, Model, Actor
Some of her works : The Hunger Games, The Hunger Games: Catching Fire, Silver Linings Playbook, The Hunger Games: Mockingjay - Part 1

Miley Cyrus

Miley Cyrus was bullied by a group of girls who called themselves the Anti-Miley Club.

Age: 24
Profession: Musician, Singer-songwriter, Actor, Voice acting, Dancer
Credits: Bolt, Justin Bieber: Never Say Never, The Last Song, Hannah Montana: The Movie

Taylor Swift

Taylor Swift says that her junior high bullies gave her the inspiration to start writing songs.

Age: 27
Profession: Guitarist, Musician, Singer-songwriter, Film Producer, Actor
Credits: The Hunger Games, San Andreas, Valentine's Day, Hannah Montana: The Movie

Tom Cruise

Tom Cruise struggled with reading, which made him an easy target for bullies.

Age: 54
Profession: Television director, Film Producer, Screenwriter, Actor
Credits: Top Gun, Mission: Impossible, Jerry Maguire, A Few Good Men

Madonna

Madonna says that the boys at her school used to bully her and call her a "hairy monster."

The Queen of Pop rebelled against her bullies by refusing to shave her armpits.

Age: 58
Profession: Record producer, Entrepreneur, Singer-songwriter, Film Producer, Screenwriter, + more
Credits: Madonna: Truth or Dare, Desperately Seeking Susan, Dick Tracy, Evita

Barack Obama

Barack Obama was bullied in school, but that didn't stop him from becoming the first African American President of the United States.

Age: 55
Profession: Politician, Author, Law professor, Writer, Lawyer
Credits: By The People: The Election of Barack Obama, 60 Minutes, Mistaken for Strangers, Senator Obama Goes to Africa

Christina Aguilera

Christina Aguilera said that she would often get ignored by her classmates because they couldn't understand her.

But she has a big dream to do something special !

Age: 36
Profession: Record producer, Entrepreneur, Singer-songwriter, Film Producer, Actor, + more
Credits: Get Smart, Moulin Rouge, Burlesque, Tony Bennett: An American Classic

Catherine, Duchess of Cambridge

The headmistress at Kate Middleton's school says that the Duchess of Cambridge was bullied for two terms.

Age: 35
Birthplace: Royal Berkshire Hospital, United Kingdom
Today, she is known by people all over the world.

Steven Spielberg

Steven Spielberg was bullied for being a "nerd" in school. Today, he is the coolest of film geeks!

Age: 70
Profession: Television director, Businessperson, Television producer, Entrepreneur, Film Producer, + more
Some of his work : Schindler's List, Saving Private Ryan, Catch Me If You Can, A.I. Artificial Intelligence and many more………..

"IT IS NOT WHERE YOU ARE NOW THAT IS IMPORTANT BUT WHERE YOU WANT TO BE BY TAKING THE RIGHT ACTIONS CONSISTENTLY UNTIL YOU REACH YOUR GOAL"

"WINNERS NEVER QUIT AND QUITTERS NEVER WIN!"

ABOUT THE AUTHOR

I started writing this book
when I was 11 years old just before
I went to high school.

I have three other sisters and one brother and
I am number three in my family.

The main thing I would love to do is help
people make good friends and I hope you
enjoy my book.

I would love to meet you one day to learn
about your special talents.

Remember :

"A STRANGER IS A FRIEND YOU HAVEN'T YET MET"

THE AUTHOR'S

CHOSEN

CHARITY

IS

UNICEF

<u>Disclaimer</u> :-

THE AUTHOR'S CHOSEN CHARITY TO FUND RAISE
FOR IS 'Unicef UK'
I am an individual taking independent actions to fund raise
vital money for Unicef's important work for children.
I am NOT endorsed by nor work for Unicef UK.
I will donate at least £1 of the proceeds from my book to
Unicef UK "

The Author's Recommended Reading List

"Leaders are Readers!"

Here are a list of great books you may want to read to give you more knowledge and information.

The Friendship Factor - Alan Loy McGinnis
How to Win Friends and Influence People –
Dale Carnegie
The Art of Dealing with People – Les Giblin
Why Men Lie and Women Cry – Allan and
Barbara Pease
Men are from Mars, Women are from Venue
- John Gray

Your Own Additional Reading List

"A SMILE
IS
ONE
THAT
THE
MORE
YOU
GIVE
AWAY
THE
MORE
YOU
WILL
GET
BACK!"

<u>Personal message from ME (Chloe)</u>
<u>to YOU MY FRIEND</u>

Remember :

"A STRANGER IS A FRIEND YOU HAVEN'T MET YET"

I BELIEVE IN YOU BECAUSE EVERYONE HAVE THEIR UNIQUE GIFTS.

DON'T ACCEPT SECOND BEST !

<u>**Thank you for reading my book.**</u>

Wishing you all the best in making friends and have a great life.

With love and best wishes.

Chloe Whiting
XXX

My other book :

"Hot Maths for Cool Kids"

I have written this book together with
my **Grampy**,

Philip Chan
aka The 10 Seconds Maths Expert

It is fun to go to different places with my Grampy.
We were at the Red Carpet Event for the Authors
Awards in London,
He received an Award for his book: The 10 Seconds
Speed Maths Technique

Other fun places we have been invited to was at
Kensington Palace, The home of the Duke and
Duchess of Cambridge, Prince William and his wife
Kate.

Other fun places like at Richard Branson's
Virgin Money Centre in London for a
charity event.

25715420R00070

Printed in Great Britain
by Amazon